ALSO BY CHARLES WRIGHT

THE
OTHER
SIDE
OF THE
RIVER

VINTAGE BOOKS

A Division of Random House

New York

THE

OTHER

SIDE

OF THE

RIVER

POEMS BY

CHARLES WRIGHT

FIRST VINTAGE BOOKS EDITION, February 1984

Copyright © 1981, 1982, 1983, 1984 by Charles Wright

Portions of this work have previously appeared in the
following publications: *The Agni Review, The Antioch
Review, Field, Paris Review, Ploughshares, Raccoon, The
Rathasker Press,* and *The Reaper.*
"Four Poems of Departure" and "Four Poems for the
New Year" first appeared in *Antaeus.*

Library of Congress Cataloging in Publication Data
Wright, Charles, 1935–
   The other side of the river.
   I. Title.
[PS3573.R5208 1984c]   811'.54   83-13729
ISBN 0-394-72367-8 (pbk.)

Manufactured in the United States of America

—GIANCARLO AND BABY, NICOLA, ALEX . . .

CONTENTS

IV

PART
ONE

LOST BODIES

Last night I thought of Torri del Benaco again,
Its almond trees in blossom,
                          its cypresses clothed in their dark fire,

And the words carved on that concrete cross

I passed each day of my life
In Kingsport going to town
  GET RIGHT WITH GOD / JESUS IS COMING SOON

If I had it all to do over again
                          I'd be a Medievalist.
I'd thoroughly purge my own floor.

Something's for sure in the clouds, but it's not for me,

Though all the while that light tips the fast-moving water,
East wind in a rush through the almond trees.
                    ———————

The cross was opposite Fleenor's Cabins below the hill
On US 11W.
Harold Shipley told me, when I was 12,
                          he'd seen a woman undressed

In the back seat of a Buick, between two men,
                          her cunt shaved clean,
In front of the motel office.
They gave him a dollar, he said, to stick his finger up there.

What can you say to that?

everything Jesus promised,

(My five senses waiting apart in their grey hoods,
Touching their beads,

licking the ashes that stained their lips)

And someone to tell it to.

———

Torri del Benaco, on the east side of Lake Garda,
Was north past Peschiera and San Vigilio,

under the Bardolino hills.
I seldom went there, and remember it poorly.

One Sunday, I drove through town on my way to Riva at the
top of the lake.
An east wind was blowing out toward the water,

Down through the vineyards, and down through the trees at
the lake's edge.

I remember the cypress nods in its warm breath.
I remember the almond blossoms

floating out on the waves, west to Salò.
I remember the way they looked there,

a small flotilla of matches.

I remember their flash in the sun's flare.

———

You've got to sign your name to something, it seems to me.
And so we rephrase the questions
Endlessly,

hoping the answer might somehow change.

Still, a piece of his heart is not a piece of your heart,

Sweet Jesus, and never will be, but stays
A little window into the past,

increasingly licked transparent
And out of shape.

When you die, you fall down,

you don't rise up
Like a scrap of burnt paper into the everlasting.
Each morning we learn this painfully,

pulling our bodies up by the roots from their deep sleep.

———————

Nobody takes that road now.

The tourist cabins are gone,
And Harold, and Rose Dials
Who lived in a tarpaper shack just off the highway,
Nailed hard to the mountainside.

And the two men and the Buick too,
Long gone down the Interstate
And the satellites that have taken us all from town.

Only the cross is still there, sunk deeper into the red clay
Than anyone could have set it.

And that luminous, nameless body whose flesh takes on
The mottoes we say we live by . . .

———————

Of all the places around the lake,

I've loved Sirmione best,
Its brilliant winks in the sun
And glassy exceptions like a trace in the mind.

Others stay in the memory like pieces of songs
You think you remember but don't,

only a phrase here and there
Surfacing as it should, and in tune.

Gardone and Desenzano are like that, and Torri del Benaco.

Mostly what I remember is one garden, outside the town of
  Garda,
Between the lake's edge and the road:
Corn and beans, it looked like, and squash and finocchio.

———————

All things that come to him come under his feet
In a glorious body,
                    they say. And why not?
It beats the alternative, the mighty working
Set to subdue the celestial flesh.

And does so, letting the grass go stiff, and the needles brown,

Letting the dirt take over. This is as far as it goes,
Where deer browse the understory and jays
                              leap through the trees,

Where chainsaws
Whittle away at the darkness, and diesel rigs
Carry our deaths all night through the endless rain.

LOST SOULS

From the bad eye and early morning
                              you raise me
Unshuttered from the body of ashes
                              you raise me
Out of the dust and moth light
                         memory
Into the undertow of my own life
                              you make me remember

────────

I never dreamed of anything as a child.
I just assumed it was all next door,
                         or day-after-tomorrow at least,
A different shirt I'd put on when the time was right.

It hasn't worked out that way.

My father wrote out his dreams on lined paper, as I do now,
And gave them up to the priest
                              for both to come to terms with.
I give you mine for the same reason,

To summon the spirits up and set the body to music.

────────

The last time I saw George Vaughan,
He was standing in front of my father's casket at the laying
    out,
One of the kindest men I've ever known.

When I was 16, he taught me the way to use a jackhammer,
                                   putting the hand grip

Into my stomach and clinching down,
Riding it out till the jarring became a straight line.

He taught me the way a shovel breathes,
And how the red clay gives away nothing.
He took my hand when my hand needed taking.

And I didn't even remember his name.

———————

One evening in 1957 I found myself outside of Nashville,
                                    face down on the ground,
A straw in my mouth, the straw stuck deep
In the ginned heart of a watermelon,
                        the faces of five friends
Almost touching my face
As we sucked the sweet gin as fast as we could.

Over the green hinge of the Cumberland Plateau
The eyelash dusk of July was coming down
                        effortlessly, smooth as an oiled joint.
Agnes rolled over and looked up at the sky.
Her cousin, our host, rolled over and looked up at the sky.

What a life, he said. Jesus, he said, what a life.

———————

Nobody needs to remember the Kingsport *Times-News*
In the summer of 1953,
                        but I do,
Disguised to myself as a newspaperman on my slow way
To the city jail to check the drunk tank,
                        full summer and after supper,
Korea just over, the neon of Wallace's News and Parks-Belk
Lying along the sidewalk like tear sheets of tinted plastic,
Across Center and down to Freel's Drug,
                        then left, and then left again

Into the blowing shadow and light
Under the elm trees,
The world and its disregard in the palm of my hand.

Nobody needs to remember the smell of bay rum
And disinfectant,
                        the desperate grey faces
Of dirt farmers caught in the wrong dark at the wrong time,
Bib overalls sour with sweat and high water,
Brogans cracked and half broken,
                                    the residue
Of all our illuminations and unnamed lives . . .
At least I thought that then.
And nobody needs to remember any of that,
                                    but I do.

———————

What *does* one do with one's life? A shelf-and-a-half
Of magazines, pictures on all the walls
Of the way I was, and everyone standing next to me?
This one, for instance for instance for instance . . .

Nothing's like anything else in the long run.
Nothing you write down is ever as true as you think it was.

But so what? Churchill and I and Bill Ring
Will still be chasing that same dead pintail duck
                            down the same rapids in 1951
Of the Holston River. And Ted Glynn
Will be running too.
                        And 1951 will always be 1951.

———————

A little curtain of flesh, Blake said,
For his own reasons . . .
And I had mine to draw it last night on the Wasatch Range

And pull it back as the sun rose
                          over the north fork
And blue weave of the Cumberlands.
It was June again, and 1964 again,
                          and I still wasn't there
As they laid her down and my father turned away,
I still imagine, precisely, into the cave of cold air
He lived in for eight more years, the cars
Below my window in Rome honking maniacally
                          O still small voice of calm . . .

LONESOME PINE SPECIAL

"I was walking out this morning with rambling on my mind."

—Sara Carter

There's a curve in the road, and a slow curve in the land,
Outside of Barbourville, Kentucky, on US 25E,
I've always liked
                    each time I've passed it,
Bottom land, river against a ridge to the west,
A few farmhouses on each side of the road, some mailboxes
Next to a dirt lane that leads off through the fields.
Each time I'd think
                    How pleasant it must be to live here.

―――――――

In Kingsport, when I was growing up,
Everyone seemed to go to Big Stone Gap, Virginia, up US 23,
All the time.
                    Everyone had an uncle or aunt there,
Or played golf, or traded cars.
They were always going up there
                                    to get married, or get liquor,
Or to get what was owed them
By someone they'd been in the service with.

Lone went up there more often than anyone else did,
Part of his territory for State Farm,
                                    somebody said,
Without much conviction.

When the talk turned to whiskey,
                                    and everyone dusted his best lie off,
We all knew, or thought we knew, where Lone went

With his funny walk and broken back
He could hit a golf ball a ton with,
                              even if he did stand sideways
Like a man hauling a body out of the water,
Being the real owner, we thought, of that gas station out on
   the Jonesboro highway
You went to the back of
                    for a pint after 10 P.M.,
Lone getting richer and richer until the Moose Lodge
Started to take his business away
                    by doing it legal, and during the daylight.

So Lone went back, we all thought,
To stumping around the golf course, still
Hitting it sideways, still selling whatever he could
To anyone foolish enough to play him and pay him,
Old Lone, slicker than owl oil.

_____

It was all so American,
The picket fence of wrought iron a hundred years old,
Lilacs at every corner of the lawned yard
                              in great heaps and folds,
A white house and wild alfalfa in scattered knots
Between the fence and the cracked sidewalk,
The wind from the Sawtooth Mountains
                    riffling the dust in slow eddies along the street
Near the end of June in Hailey, Idaho,
The house where Pound was born,
                              with its red maple floors
And small windows two blocks from Idaho 75,
Hemingway ten miles on up the same road between two
   evergreens,
Nobody noticing either place
                              as the cars went through town
All night and all day, going north, going south . . .

Another landscape I liked
Was south of Wytheville, Virginia, on US 52
Just short of the Carolina line,
                              a steel bridge over the New River,
Pasture on both sides of the road and woods on the easy
    slopes,
Big shrubs and trees lining the river banks like fur,
The road and the river both
Angling back toward the Iron Mountains,
The valley bulging out to the east
                              in a graceful swirl,
The dead chestnut trees like grey candles
Wherever the woods began . . .

What is it about a known landscape
                              that tends to undo us,
That shuffles and picks us out
For terminal demarcation, the way a field of lupine
Seen in profusion deep in the timber
Suddenly seems to rise like a lavender ground fog
At noon?
        What is it inside the imagination that keeps surprising us
At odd moments
                when something is given back
We didn't know we had had
In solitude, spontaneously, and with great joy?

────────

Today, at midsummer noon, I took the wooden floats
To the Yaak River, the small ones I'd carved from the larch
And cedar chips,
                and loosed them downstream
To carry my sins away, as the palace guardians did each year
    at this time
in medieval Japan,

Where the river goes under the new bridge

                                   on County 508
And the first homesteaders took up their quarter sections.
From Sam Runyan's to Susie Speed's,
Through white water and rock and the tendrilous shade
Of the tamaracks,

                     out into rubbery blotches of sunlight,
The float's shadows hanging beneath them like odd anchors
Along the pebbled bottom, the river slowing and widening,
The floats at great distances from one another
Past Binder's cabin under the black

                          of the evergreen-covered dam
And over the falls and gone into foam and next year . . .

In the world of dirt, each tactile thing

                         repeats the untouchable
In its own way, and in its own time.
Just short of Tryon, North Carolina, on US 176,
Going south down the old Saluda Grade,

                         kudzu has grown up
And over the tops of miles of oak trees and pine trees,
A wall of vines a hundred feet high, or used to be,
Into South Carolina,
That would have gone for a hundred more with the right
   scaffolding,
Rising out of the rock and hard clay in thin, prickly ropes
To snake and thread in daily measurable distances
Over anything still enough long enough,

                         and working its way
Out of the darkness and overhang of its own coils
To break again and again
Into the sunlight, worthless and everywhere,

                     breathing, breathing,
Looking for leverage and a place to climb.

—————

It's true, I think, as Kenkō says in his *Idleness,*
That all beauty depends upon disappearance,
The bitten edges of things,

                the gradual sliding away
Into tissue and memory,

            the uncertainty
And dazzling impermanence of days we beg our meanings
   from,
And their frayed loveliness.

Going west out of Kalispell, Montana on US 2,
If you turned off at Kila,

              and skirted the big slough
Where Doagie Duncan killed three men some seventy years
   ago
After a fight over muskrat hides,
Then turned south toward the timber

                 and higher ground
On the dirt road to the Flathead Mine,
Past Sundelius' homestead and up toward Brown's Meadows,
Then swung down where the mine road

            branches right and doubles back,
You'd come through the thinning spruce and fir
And lodgepole pine to the suddenly open hillsides
And deep draws

       of the Hog Heaven country
And start to see what I mean, the bunchgrass and bitterroot
And wild clover flattening under the wind
As you turned from the dirt road,

            opened the Kansas gate
And began to follow with great care
The overgrown wagon ruts through the blowing field,

             the huge tamarack snag,

Where the tracks end and the cabin is,
Black in the sunlight's wash and flow
                            just under the hill's crown,
Pulling you down like weight to the front door . . .

The cabin is still sizable, four rooms and the walls made
Of planed lumber inside,
                        the outside chinked with mud
And cement, everything fifty years
Past habitation, the whole structure
                            leaning into the hillside,
Windowless, doorless, and oddly beautiful in its desolation
And attitude, and not like
The cold and isolate misery it must have stood for
When someone lived here, and heard, at night,
This same wind sluicing the jack pines
                            and ruined apple trees
In the orchard, and felt the immensity
Loneliness brings moving under his skin
Like a live thing, and emptiness everywhere like a live thing
Beyond the window's reach and fire's glare . . .

Whoever remembers that best owns all this now.
And after him it belongs to the wind again,
            and the shivering bunchgrass, and the seed cones.
                    ————————

There is so little to say, and so much time to say it in.

Once, in 1955 on an icy road in Sam's Gap, North Carolina,
Going north into Tennessee on US 23,
I spun out on a slick patch
And the car turned once-and-a-half around,
Stopping at last with one front wheel on a rock
                            and the other on air,
Hundreds of feet of air down the mountainside

I backed away from, mortal again
After having left myself
                         and returned, having watched myself
Wrench the wheel toward the spin, as I'm doing now,
Stop and shift to reverse, as I'm doing now,
                         and back out on the road
As I entered my arms and fingers again
Calmly, as though I had never left them,
Shift to low, and never question the grace
That had put me there and alive, as I'm doing now . . .

Solo Joe is a good road.
It cuts south-west off Montana 5o8 above Blacktail Creek,
Crosses the East Fork of the Yaak River
                         and climbs toward Mt. Henry.
Joe was an early prospector
Back in the days when everything came in by pack string
Or didn't come in at all.
                         One spring he shot his pet cat
On the front porch with a rifle between the eyes
As she came through the cabin door.
He later explained she was coming for him
                         but he got her first.
He drank deer's blood, it was said, and kept to himself,
Though one story has him a gambler later downriver near
   Kalispell.
Nobody lives there now,
But people still placer mine in the summer, and camp out
Illegally on the river bank.
No one knows anything sure about Joe but his first name
And the brown government sign that remembers him.
And that's not so bad, I think.
                         It's a good road, as I say,
And worse things than that will happen to most of us.

The road in is always longer than the road out,
Even if it's the same road.
I think I'd like to find one
                    impassable by machine,
A logging road from the early part of the century,
Overgrown and barely detectable.
I'd like it to be in North Carolina,
                              in Henderson County
Between Mt. Pinnacle and Mt. Anne,
An old spur off the main track
The wagons and trucks hauled out on.
Blackberry brambles, and wild raspberry and poison ivy
Everywhere; grown trees between the faint ruts;
Deadfall and windfall and velvety sassafras fans
On both sides . . .
                    It dips downhill and I follow it.
It dips down and it disappears and I follow it.

TWO STORIES

Tonight, on the deck, the lights
Semaphore up at me through the atmosphere,
Town lights, familiar lights
                              pulsing and slacking off
The way they used to back on the ridge outside of Kingsport
35 years ago,
The moonlight sitting inside my head
Like knives,
                the cold like a drug I knew I'd settle down with.
I used to imagine them shore lights, as these are, then,
As something inside me listened with all its weight
For the sea-surge and the sea-change.

———————

There's a soft spot in everything
Our fingers touch,
                      the one place where everything breaks
When we press it just right.
The past is like that with its arduous edges and blind sides,
The whorls of our fingerprints
                                    embedded along its walls
Like fossils the sea has left behind.

———————

This is a story I swear is true.

I used to sleepwalk. But only
On camping trips,
                    or whenever I slept outside.
One August, when I was 11, on Mount LeConte in Tennessee,

Campfire over, and ghost story over,
Everyone still asleep, apparently I arose
From my sleeping bag,
                    opened the tent flap, and started out on the trail
That led to the drop-off, where the mountainside
Went straight down for almost a thousand feet.
Half-moon and cloud cover, so some light
As I went on up the path through the rhododendron,
The small pebbles and split roots
                              like nothing under my feet.
The cliffside was half a mile from the campsite.
As I got closer,
                moving blindly, unerringly,
Deeper in sleep than the shrubs,
I stepped out, it appears,
Onto the smooth lip of the rock cape of the cliff,
When my left hand, and then my right hand,
Stopped me as they were stopped
By the breathing side of a bear which woke me
And there we were,
                the child and the black bear and the cliff-drop,
And this is the way it went—
                        I stepped back, and I turned around,
And I walked down through the rhododendron
And never looked back,
                    truly awake in the throbbing world,
And I ducked through the low flap
Of the tent, so quietly, and I went to sleep
And never told anyone
Till years later when I thought I knew what it meant,
                              which now I've forgot.

                ——————

And this one is questionable,

Though sworn to me by an old friend
Who'd killed a six-foot diamondback about seven o'clock in
   the morning
(He'd found it coiled in a sunny place),
And threw it into a croker sack with its head chopped off,
                        and threw the sack in the back of a jeep,
Then left for his day's work
On the farm.
                That evening he started to show the snake
To someone, and put his hand in the sack to pull it out.
As he reached in, the snake's stump struck him.
His wrist was bruised for a week.

————————

It's not age,
           nor time with its gold eyelid and blink,
Nor dissolution in all its mimicry
That lifts us and sorts us out.
It's discontinuity
              and all its spangled coming between
That sends us apart and keeps us there in a dread.
It's what's in the rear-view mirror,
                      smaller and out of sight.

————————

What do you do when the words don't come to you anymore,
And all the embolisms fade in the dirt?
And the ocean sings in its hammock,
                rocking itself back and forth?
And you live at the end of the road where the sky starts its
   dark decline?

The barking goes on and on
                 from the far hill, constantly
Sticking its noise in my good ear.

Goodbye, Miss Sweeney, goodbye.
I'm starting to think about the psychotransference of all things.
It's small bones in the next life.
It's small bones,
               and heel and toe forever and ever.

THE OTHER SIDE OF THE RIVER

Easter again, and a small rain falls
On the mockingbird and the housefly,

                       on the Chevrolet

In its purple joy
And the TV antennas huddled across the hillside—

Easter again, and the palm trees hunch
Deeper beneath their burden,

                   the dark puddles take in

Whatever is given them,
And nothing rises more than halfway out of itself—

Easter with all its little mouths open into the rain.

———————

There is no metaphor for the spring's disgrace,
No matter how much the rose leaves look like bronze dove
   hearts,
No matter how much the plum trees preen in the wind.

For weeks I've thought about the Savannah River,
For no reason,

           and the winter fields around Garnett, South Carolina

My brother and I used to hunt
At Christmas,

          Princess and Buddy working the millet stands

And the vine-lipped face of the pine woods
In their languorous zig-zags,
The quail, when they flushed, bursting like shrapnel points
Between the trees and the leggy shrubs

                   into the undergrowth,

Everything else in motion as though under water,
My brother and I, the guns, their reports tolling from far away
Through the aqueous, limb-filtered light,
December sun like a single tropical fish
Uninterested anyway,
                              suspended and holding still
In the coral stems of the pearl-dusked and distant trees . . .

There is no metaphor for any of this,
Or the meta-weather of April,
The vinca blossoms like deep bruises among the green.

———————

It's linkage I'm talking about,
                    and harmonies and structures
And all the various things that lock our wrists to the past.

Something infinite behind everything appears,
                              and then disappears.

It's all a matter of how
                    you narrow the surfaces.
It's all a matter of how you fit in the sky.

———————

Often, at night, when the stars seem as close as they do now,
   and as full,
And the trees balloon and subside in the way they do
                              when the wind is right,
As they do now after the rain,
                    the sea way off with its false sheen,
And the sky that slick black of wet rubber,
I'm 15 again, and back on Mt. Anne in North Carolina
Repairing the fire tower,
Nobody else around but the horse I packed in with,
                    and five days to finish the job.

Those nights were the longest nights I ever remember,
The lake and pavilion 3,000 feet below
                                    as though modeled in tinfoil,
And even more distant than that,
The last fire out, the after-reflection of Lake Llewellyn
Aluminum glare in the sponged dark,
Lightning bugs everywhere,
                                    the plump stars
Dangling and falling near on their black strings.

These nights are like that,
The silvery alphabet of the sea
                                    increasingly difficult to transcribe,
And larger each year, everything farther away, and less clear,
Than I want it to be,
                                    not enough time to do the job,
And faint thunks in the earth,
As though somewhere nearby a horse was nervously pawing
   the ground.

I want to sit by the bank of the river,
                                    in the shade of the evergreen tree,
And look in the face of whatever,
                                    the whatever that's waiting for me.

There comes a point when everything starts to dust away
More quickly than it appears,
                                    when what we have to comfort the dark
Is just that dust, and just its going away.

25 years ago I used to sit on this jut of rocks
As the sun went down like an offering through the glaze
And backfires of Monterey Bay,

And anything I could think of was mine because it was there
                              in front of me, numinously everywhere,
Appearing and piling up . . .

So to have come to this,
                    remembering what I did do, and what I
                    didn't do,
The gulls whimpering over the boathouse,
                                        the monarch butterflies
Cruising the flower beds,
And all the soft hairs of spring thrusting up through the wind,
And the sun, as it always does,
                    dropping into its slot without a click,
Is a short life of trouble.

PART
TWO

HOMAGE TO CLAUDE LORRAINE

I had a picture by him—a print, I think—on my bedroom wall
In Verona in 1959,
                              via Anzani n. 3.
Or maybe a drawing, a rigged ship in a huge sea,
Storm waves like flames above my bed.
It's lost between there and here now,
                                        and has been for years,
Trapped in the past's foliage, as so much else is
In spite of our constancy, or how
We rattle the branches and keep our lights on the right place.

The room had a vaulted ceiling and faced east.
The living room was a tower with skylights on four sides.
A third room sloped with the roof
                              until it was two feet high at the far wall,
All of this part of a reconstructed attic, and washed white.

I lived there for two years,
                              one block from the Adige
Where seagulls, like little loaves of fresh bread,
Drifted and turned on its grey coils.
Between the sea fires of Claude Lorraine
                              and the curled sheets of the river,
I burned on my swivel stool
Night after night,
                    looking into the future, its charred edges
Holding my life like a frame
I'd hope to fit into one day, unsigned and rigged for the deeps.

MANTOVA

Mantegna on all the walls,
The Mincio puddled outside the gates,
                            clouds tattooed on its blue chest,
Mantova floats in the pigeon-light of late afternoon
Twenty-two years ago.
Rain shoots its white cuffs across the scene.

I remember a dream I had once in Mantova,
Everyone in it in full dress,
                            refectory hall,
Goblets and white linen.
At the near end of the table, heaped on a bronze salver
Like quail, all wishbone and delicate leg,
The roast children were served up.
                                    "You must try the thighs,"
My host said, his gloves still on.
                            "You must try the thighs."

Half the sky full of rain, and half not,
Reeds under water pressure to stay still,
The river oncoming but not flashed,
Everything upside down,
                            the sky at rest underfoot.
Words, but who can remember?

What words does the sky know, or the clouds know?

On the wall of the summer house,
                            where Giulio Romano left him,
The lion sips at the river bank, and the trees provide.

DRIVING TO PASSALACQUA, 1960

The road is a hard road,
                    and the river is wadded and flattened out
Due west of Santa Maria dell'Ortolo.
Each morning I drove with its steady breathing right to my
    right,
Dawn like a courtier
With his high white hat just coming into the room,
Ponte Pietra cut in the morning gauze,
                                    Catullus off to my left
Released in the labials of the sunlight,
Fire on the water,
                    daylight striking its match
Wherever it pleased
Along the Adige and stitched cross-tiles of San Fermo . . .

What do I do with all this?
                    Phlegethon
He must have crossed,
                    Dante, I mean,
His cloak like a net as he glided and stepped over the stones.
I hurry on by, breakfast
In mind, and the day's duty, half-left at the *bivio*.
Our outfit was out in town,
                    in hiding, spiked fence and three Chevrolets
In front when I pulled up for roll call
And the morning mail and settling in,
DiCenzo signed out for Udine, and Joe for Vienna.
All day the river burned by my desk
                    as I sailed my boats down its licks for a foot or so.

THREE POEMS OF DEPARTURE

1

Sitting again on the front porch of the first cabin.
Grind of the deerfly, hone of the bee.
Someone is mourning inconsolably somewhere else.
Yellow of goldenrod, bronze of the grass.
By the creek bridge, the aspen leaves are waving goodbye,
   goodbye.
Silence of paint brush and cow pink.
Take the dirt from the old trail up in your hand, Pilgrim,
                    and throw it into the wind.

2

The meadow surrounds us on three sides,
Steep woods to the north;
It's fifty-one miles downriver to where the highway begins.
I leave by the opposite way,
               over the summit
Through deadfall and clear cut and shell-shot snow of July.

Already sundown has passed you and follows me up the road,
Color of dragonfly wings.
On the other side, as I start down,
                  it passes me too,
Your voice now flat as a handkerchief
Folded away for miles in its pine drawer.

3

28 August and first frost
Like a horizon across the meadow.
                          The yellow top
Of the signal tamarack
Sticks up like a stalk of goldenrod from the southern
   mountain,
Autumn starting to pull in its heavy net.

Thistle spores tumble like star-webs between the trees.
The slough grass is brown in the dry channels.
Tomorrow we leave for the desert,
                          almost two thousand miles away.
But tonight, under the white eye of Betelgeuse,
We'll point out the pony stars, and their gusty hooves.

ITALIAN DAYS

1

Thinking again of a weekend trip to Ferrara,
Cosimo Tura on one wall,
                Miss d'Este long gone from the next,
I took from Verona once,
A place where the streets were as wide as Parisian boulevards,
The Po like a frayed rope out past the bulge of the dikes.

The weekend before I'd been to Merano and back,
And almost become a squib
                in the *Stars & Stripes*
When the helicopter's engine stopped
Thousands of feet above the Brenner highway,
And we began to slide sideways down the air
As quietly as a snowflake,
                the huge rotary blades above us
Circling like paddle churns in the wind

Languidly,
           the stillness abrupt, the plane
In a long slip like a scimitar curve toward the ground
Rising to meet us, its trees
Focusing automatically larger with each look
As though raised through a microscope,
The engine catching at last on its last turn,
Pine branches less than fifty feet below us,
                the blade-slide bottoming out

As we started to rise and swing north
Up the Val d'Adige and into the emerald sundown
Outside Merano . . .
                          Back up out of darkness an hour later,
The houses beginning to flash on like matches below,
Left over Trento and left over Schio
                          and down, everyone out to supper,
The waitress admonishing Manzolin, *"Non si taglia la pasta."*

Cut to Ferrara, and me
Threading my way out of town through bicycles, Vespas and
    runty Fiats
South to Ravenna and Rimini,
                          the lap of the Adriatic
And western Byzantium
In the long grasses of S. Apollinare in Classe,
The field stubble gold in the noon sun.

Cut to Verona, the town I always left from,
Work over, and Happy Hour,
                          Modugno on every phonograph
On Via Mazzini, *"Ciao, ciao, bambina . . ."*
It's 1959 and after supper,
Everyone disappearing like rain
From the streets and Caffè Dante, the fog in,
Can Grande skulking and disappearing in marble above his
    tomb

As I do along the cobblestones
He grins down on,
                          gone through the fog toward S. Anastasia
And the Due Torri, everything swaddled as though in
    newsprint,
The river off to the right like a licking sound,

Up past the Duomo,
                    then right and across the last bridge,
Where the beggar loomed in her burning chair.
Each night as I passed her
                    it took a hundred lire to put out the fire.

Up north, in the watersheds and rock slides of the Dolomites,
Snow has been leaving its same message
For thousands of years
                    on the bark of the cedar trees.
There is no stopping the comings and goings in this world,
No stopping them, to and fro.

2

Palladio's buildings shone like the collar on someone's dog
In Vicenza, the only inscript in all the town.
For the rest, it was Goldstein patrolling the avenues
At sundown with hot hands.
                    And Venezia, Lord of the Bees,
In the dark hives of the Hotel Artù with hot hands.
It was Charles with hot hands,
His fingers on this and that wherever he turned
In the bars of Little America.
It was weekend and off-duty and kicking the gong
In a foreign country,
                    left foot and right foot.

Sister water, brother fire, gentle my way
Across,
        one foot on the river, one foot in the flames,
My lack of ability to remember it right.
The time we spotted the Vicentine,
For instance, it rained and dimpled all the way back,

With Grace in his lap and him driving,
Sneezing and making amends.

On alternate Sundays we'd drive to Soave and Asolo,
Padova and the Euganean Hills,
Always looking for the event,
                    not knowing that we were it.

This was the world we lived in,
And couldn't get shut of.
                    And these were the rocks we walked on,
Milano, Certosa, footstep
                    after footstep echoing down the galleries,
Goldstein checking the nuns out,
Venezia settling like smoke at the unbitten center of things.
One Sunday after the Trattoria La Brera,
We went to Scuderi's place, his huge canvases
Stacked like Sheetrock against the wall.
                    "I have to keep them like this,"
He said, "to keep my life in order."
He died the next winter,
            the heater electrocuting him in the bathtub.

Some nights, when the stars flash their gang codes,
And the fog slides in as cautiously as a bride
Across the steps the trees make
                    up from the sea,
And the gnatlight starts to solidify
Like a crust on the palm leaf and the pepper switch,
And the smell of the paper-whites
                    hangs like a June garden
Above the kitchen table,
Scuderi calls out my name
                    as I climb the six flights to his room

And stand in the doorway again,
Electric and redivivus in the world of light

He lived in inside his paintings for all those years,
Vaseline light
                    through the slow filter of late November,
Acid light off the north Italian lakes,
Shorthand of light from the olive leaves
                              as they turn and tick in the wind,
Last light of the *dopoguerra* lifting Milan like a ship
In the Lombardy night outside his window
On top of the city wall,
                          bar light and aftermath,
Scuderi whitening to grain-out and then to blank,
Light like a sheet of paper
Everywhere, flat and unwrinkled and unreturnable.

3

At the end of the last word,
When night comes walking across the lake on its hands,
And nothing appears in the mirror,
                              or has turned to water
Where nothing walks or lies down,
What will your question be,
Whistling the dogs of mold in, giving them meat?
And what will it profit you?

No thought of that back then,
Bivouacked outside the castle above Marostica
Whose walls
                    downswept and pinioned the town like wings
In its coming-to-rest,
                          the town square

Blocked out like a chessboard black and white,
Black and white from up there,
Where the rook looked down on the knight's play.

What eschatology of desire
                              could move us in those days,
What new episiotomy of the word?
At San Gimignano, outside of town,
I did see that no one could last for good,
That no one could answer back from the other side.
Still, I'd like to think I've learned how to speak to them,
I'd like to think I know how to conjugate
                              "Can you hear me?" and "What?"

In Rome, on the Via Cassia,
                    there was opportunity enough
For that in the catacombs,
                    the lost bodies slipped in their slots
Like letters someone had never answered,
And then tossed out,
A chance to step back from the light
                              of the strung electric bulb,
And ask again if our first day in the dark
Is our comfort or signature.

Most of what I remember
Has nothing to do with any of that, it turns out:
A view from the Pinacoteca window across Siena
One morning in 1959
                              and out to the hillscapes and olive shine;
The way Piero della Francesca's *Madonna del Parto*
Was leaning against the wall
                              in Monterchi, and still unlit;
The eel fisherman that May twilight along the Mincio River.

But Scuderi did, and the helicopter did,
And the full moon like Borso's skull on the Zattere,
Fog smoking up from the humped lagoon;
                              and Eve coming out of Adam's rib
On San Zeno's doors in Verona,
                              her foot still stuck in his side;
And the morning we sat on the terrace,
                              Jim Gates and Tom Fucile and I,
In Bassano, the bowler of Monte Grappa across the valley,
Ghost hat on the head of northern Italy.

There is, in the orchards of Sommacampagna,
A sleet-like and tenuous iridescence that falls
Through the peach trees whenever it rains.
                              The blossoms parachute to the ground
So heavy and so distinct,
And the light above Riva spokes out from under the clouds
Like Blake,
        the wires for the grapevines beading their little rainbows,
The cars planing by on the highway,
                              shooshing their golden plumes . . .

What gifts there are are all here, in this world.

THREE POEMS FOR THE NEW YEAR

1

I have nothing to say about the way the sky tilts
Toward the absolute,
                        or why I live at the edge
Of the black boundary,
                        a continent where the waves
Counsel my coming in and my going out.

I have nothing to say about the brightness and drear
Of any of that, or the vanity
                        of our separate consolations.
I have nothing to say about the companies of held breath.

All year I have sung in vain,
Like a face breaking up in the font of holy water,
                        not hungry, not pure of heart.
All year as my body, sweet pilgrimage,
                        moved from the dark to the dark.

What true advice the cicada leaves.

2

How strange it is to awake
Into middle age, Rimbaud left blue and out cold

In the snow,
              the Alps wriggling away to a line
In the near distance,
                          someone you don't know
Coming to get your body, revive it, and arrange for the train.

How strange to awake to that,

The windows all fogged with breath,
The landscape outside in a flash,
                              and gone like a scarf
On the neck of someone else,
                          so white, so immaculate,
The deserts and caravans
Hanging like Christmas birds in the ice-dangled evergreens.

3

All day at the window seat
                          looking out, the red knots

Of winter hibiscus deep in the foregreen,
Slick globes of oranges in the next yard,
Many oranges,
              and slow winks in the lemon trees
Down the street, slow winks when the wind blows the leaves
    back.

The ache for fame is a thick dust and weariness in the heart.

All day with the knuckle of solitude
To gnaw on,
              the turkey buzzards and red-tailed hawk

Lifting and widening concentrically over the field,
Brush-tails of the pepper branches

                          writing invisibly on the sky . . .

The ache for anything is a thick dust in the heart.

ROMA I

To start with, it looked abstract
                            that first year from the balcony
Over the Via del Babuino,
Local color as far as the eye could see,
                        and mumbled in slaps and clumps
Of gouaches constantly to itself,
A gentian snood of twilight in winter,
                            blood orange in spring,
And ten thousand yards of glass in the summer sky.
Wherever you looked in October, the night was jigged.

(In front of the Ristorante Bolognese,
Monica Vitti and Michelangelo Antonioni are having an
    aperitif,
Watched by a hundred people.
                            On the marble plaque
On the building across the street from my room to the Polish
    patriot
Whose name escapes me forever,
The words start to disappear in the April nightswell.
The river of cars turns its small lights on,
                and everyone keeps on looking at everyone else.)

Rome in Rome? We're all leading afterlives
                            of one sort or another,
Wrapped in bird feathers, pecking away at our gathered seed,
The form inside the form inside.
And nothing's more common by now than the obelisk

At one end of the street
                        and the stone boat at the other . . .
The smell of a dozen dinners is borne up
On exhaust fumes,
                timeless, somehow, and vaguely reassuring.

ROMA II

I looked long and long at my mother's miniature
The next year,
                        the year I lived on the east side
Of the church building that overlooked the Campo dei Fiori.
Her body had entered the oak grove.
By the river of five-sided leaves she had laid it down,
Hummingbird hard at the yellow shells of the sour grass,
Red throat in the light vouchsafed,
                        then quick hum to a marigold.

The poem is a self-portrait
                        always, no matter what mask
You take off and put back on.
As this one is, color of cream and a mouthful of air.
Rome is like that, and we are,
                        taken off and put back on.
Downstairs, in front of the *Pollarolla*,
The Irish poets are sketching themselves in,
                        and the blue awnings, and motorbikes.
They draw till we're all in, even our hands.

Surely, as has been said, emptiness is the beginning of all
    things.
Thus wind over water,
                        thus tide-pull and sand-sheen
When the sea turns its lips back . . .
Still, we stand by the tree whose limbs branch out like bones,
Or steps in the bronchial sediment.
And the masters stand in their azure gowns,
Sticks in their hands, palm leaves like birds above their heads.

HOMAGE TO CESARE PAVESE

Death will come and it will have your eyes
From morning to morning, sleepless,

                     an old remorse.
Your eyes will be vain words, a silence
You'll see as you lean out to the mirror
Each day,

        the one look that it has for everyone.

It will be like ooze from the sea,
Like stopping a vice

            and the sin. It will be like stopping the sin.
It will be the dead face in the mirror
Listening to shut lips.
It will descend silently,

           speechlessly into whirlpools.

Death will come and it will have your eyes,
Ridiculous vice

        and the same look.
You are the great weariness.
You are scorched and burned back by the sea.
You say nothing,

        and nobody speaks to you.

This is a balance sheet and the names don't count.
One nail on top of another,

           four nails make a cross.
Nothing can add to the past—
Woman is as woman does,

          and night is always the night.
With its black heart and its black hands it lays me down.

PART

THREE

CRYOPEXY

Looming and phosphorescent against the dark,
Words, always words.
                      What language does light speak?
Vowels hang down from the pepper tree
                         in their green and their gold.

———————

The star charts and galactic blood trails behind the eye
Where the lights are, and the links and chains are,
                       cut wall through ascending wall,
Indigo corridors, the intolerable shine
                    transgressing heaven's borders . . .

———————

What are the colors of true splendor,
                        yellow and white,
Carnation and ivory, petal and bone?
Everything comes from fire.

———————

Glare and glare-white,
                   light like a plate of isinglass
Under the lid,
             currents of fox-fire between the layers,
And black dots like the blood bees of Paradise . . .

———————

Radiance comes through the eye
                and lodges like cut glass in the mind,
Never vice versa,
Somatic and self-contained.

———————

Like soiled stars from the night-blooming jasmine vine
Espaliered against the sky,
               char flakes rise from their blank deeps

Through peach light and apricot
Into the endlessness behind the eye.

––––––––

Blood clots, like numb houseflies, hang
In the alabaster and tracery,
                              icy detritus
Rocked in the swish and tug
                  of the eye's twice-turned and moonless tides.
Behind them, tourmaline thread-ladders
Web up through the nothingness,
                    the diamond and infinite glare . . .

––––––––

Weightlessness underwrites everything
In the deep space of the eye,
                    the wash and drift of oblivion
Sifting the color out,
                    polishing, still polishing
Long after translucence comes.

––––––––

One black, electric blot, blood-blown,
Vanishes like Eurydice
                    away from the light's mouth
And under the vitreous bulge of the eye's hill,
Down, O down, down . . .

––––––––

Clocking the slurs and back-lit snow
In their dark descent:
A Vaseline-colored medicine cloud floats to the left,
A comet-like shadow-slur floats to the right
Through a different throb,
                    the snow in its quartzed downfall.

––––––––

Sometimes, in the saffron undercurrents
                    trailing like Buddhist prayer robes

Across the eye,
                    clear eels and anemones
Bob and circle and sink back through the folds,
Caught in the sleeve of the curl's turn.

                    ————————

Across the eye's Pacific, stars
                    drop in the black water like pursed lips,
Islands and tiny boats
Dipping under the white lid of the strung horizon,
                    this one in amethyst, this one in flame.

T'ANG NOTEBOOK

Fine clouds open their outfits

                and show us their buttons.
Moonlight widens the waves.
Step on your own song and listen to mine,
Not bitter like yours,

                not flicked raw by lashes of dust.
Already, over Italy, the cold sun rises.

How I would like a mountain

           if I had means enough to live as a recluse.
I would like to renounce it all
And turn toward the ash-gold of flame

             mullioned between the palm fronds.

That constellation, with its seven high stars,

             is lifting its sword in the midnight.
I love you, dog, I love you.

Remain here and lengthen your days,

                Pilgrim,
Fame is a mist of grief on the river waves . . .

The low, wet clouds move faster than you do,
Snowed moon, your jade hair sleet

             and grown thin.
All night I ask what time it is.

Stories of passion make sweet dust . . .
Sunset like a girl's robe falling away long ago . . .
An old song handles my heart . . .

Outside the side door, a luck-spider,
                    huge in the flashlight's lamp,
Rappels down the air
              to single a stitch and make her starred bed.
In the dark past the hemlock, something with small, bright
  wings
Has come from a great distance, and is tired
                          and wants to lie down.

_____

Night spreads its handful of star-clusters and one eclipse
Above the palm tree.
There are shuddering birds and dead grasses
Wherever I turn my face.

_____

The ten thousand star-fish caught in the net of heaven
Flash at the sky's end.
Gulls settle, like grains of dust, on the black sand.
Lady of Light, Donna Dolorosa,
                    you drift like a skeleton
Through the night clouds.
The surf comes in and goes out like smoke.
Give me a sign,
            show me the blessing pierced in my side.

_____

This wind that comes in off the Pacific,
Where the color of mountains both is and is not,
                    ripples the distant marsh grass
And the grey doors of the sea.
The evening begins to close like a morning-glory.
Like fear in a little boat,
            the light slips under the sky.

_____

When the mind is loosened and borne up,
The body is lightened
              and feels it too could float in the wind,
A bell-sound between here and sleep.

————————

A water egret planes down like a page of blank paper
Toward the edge of the noon sky.
              Let me, like him, find an island of white reeds
To settle down on, under the wind, forgetting words.

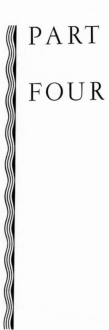

PART

FOUR

ARKANSAS TRAVELLER

On the far side of the water, high on a sand bar,
Grandfathers are lolling above the Arkansas River,
Guitars in their laps, cloth caps like Cagney down over their
    eyes.
A woman is strumming a banjo.
                        Another adjusts her bow tie
And boiled shirtwaist.
And in the half-light the frogs begin from their sleep
To ascend into darkness,
Vespers recalibrate through the underbrush,
                            the insect choir

Offering its clear soprano
Out of the vaulted gum trees into the stained glass of the sky.

—————

Almost 95 years to the day I saw
Ellison Smythe passed out
                  on the back seat of an Oldsmobile 88
In the spring of 1952 in Biltmore Forest, N.C.,
Who then rose up from the dark of his 16th year
And said to the nothingness:
                     Where are we,
Who's driving this goddamn thing?
My great-grandfather stepped off the boat
                  from the archduchy of Upper Austria
And headed north to the territory.
And into another war
               here, just past the Mississippi,
On the Arkansas.
             I don't know that it was such a great blessing
Sending us to Arkansas,

But it was so regarded at the time, and we're grateful to Gen.
  Jackson.
Still, don't let me die as grandmother did,
                              suddenly on a steamboat
Stuck fast on a sand bar unable to get to Little Rock.
And was four years later a volunteer captain
In the Confederacy,
                    and took a Minie ball in his palate
At Chickamauga he carried there till his death
Almost half a century afterwards.

                              And wrote a poem back
To the widow of one of his men about a sure return
"Where life is not a breath,
Nor life's affections, transient fire . . . in heaven's light."
And was captured again,
                    and wounded again, confined for two years
At Rock Island prison.
And came back to Little Rock and *began his career.*
And died at 66,
          a ticket to Cuba stored flat in his jacket pocket.

———————

When Jesus walked on the night grass
                    they say not even the dew trembled.
Such intricate catechisms of desire.
Such golden cars down the wrong side of the sky.

———————

Each summer in Little Rock,
                    like a monk in his cell
Saying the lesson over and over
Until it is shining, all day I'd prove up my childhood till lights
  out
Snapped on the fireflies who floated
Like miniature jellyfish
                    off the reefs of the sleeping porch

Whose jasmine and rose-scented air broke over me back and
   forth
Before I could count the half of them,
                              and settled me under.

This was before I was 10.
That year my grandfather, my look-alike on the sand bar, died,
The war ended, and nothing was ever the same way
Again.
        His mantelpiece clock sits on my dresser now,
Still gilded and 19th century.
Devotion, remember, is what counts.
Without it you're exiled, twisted and small.

————————

The next morning we'd play golf,
                        four holes on the back side,
Trailing our footprints like paired bodies emptied and left out
   to dry
In the web of sunlight and wet grass
                        behind us over the clipped fairways,
My grandmother and I up before anyone else
Each day I was there,
                  the sun already a huge, hot thumb
At 7 o'clock on our bare heads.
Later, its print still warm on my forehead,
Sunset like carrot juice down the left pane of the sky
Into the indeterminacy of somewhere else,
I'd roll the tarpaulin down and up
On the sleeping porch,
                  the frog-shrill and the insect-shrill
Threading out of the bushes
                        as palpable as a heartstring,
Whatever that was back then, always in memory . . .

————————

To speak of the dead is to make them live again:
                        we invent what we need.

Knot by knot I untie myself from the past
And let it rise away from me like a balloon.
What a small thing it becomes.
What a bright tweak at the vanishing point, blue on
    blue.

TO GIACOMO LEOPARDI IN THE SKY

If you are become an eternal idea,
Refusing investiture in our pink rags,
                          wise beyond body and form,
Or if you housel elsewhere a different sun
In one of the other aethers,
                          from down here
Where our years are fanged and omnivorous,
Listen to what these words say, from one who remembers you.

———————

July 17th, on the front deck
Looking out through the slats and palm leaves,
The ocean horizonless and sending out signals,
I start to unmarble
                    interminable spaces beyond it,
Silences so immense they sound like wind,
Like this wind that dismays me
With its calm
              as it pulls the sheet of the night
Over my head.
How sweet it is to drown in such sure water.

———————

Whenever I see you
On your left side through the clouds
Looking down on us,
                    our tongues tied, our friends all gone,
Our hearts and breaths with the air let out of them,
You make me bitter for being so much like you.

———————

What day did I take this picture you have no part in?
1959, no leaves on the trees, late fall.
                          Ponte Pietra over the Adige.

Verona, early morning.
What purpose your brief drifting along my course?
You try to erase your tracks
                              but you're too far from the ground.
You've throbbed enough.
Everything on the earth is worth your sighs.

————————

Never to see the light is best, you say,
                              who were made for joy,
Your neck of chalk like a vapor trail across the sky.

————————

I know you're up there, hiding behind the noon light
And the crystal of space.
                    Down here,
In the lurch and gasp the day makes as it waits for you
In your black suit and mother-of-pearl,
The mail comes, the garbage goes,
                              the paired butterflies
Dip and swoop in formation,
Bees trail their tongues
                    and tiptoe around the circumferences
Of the melaleuca puffs,
Sucking the sweetness up, July 27th,
The hummingbird asleep on her branch,
                              the spider drawn up in flame.

————————

You kept reading and reading,
Vowel over consonant
                        then three steps to the stars,
And there you languish,
                    outlined in flash points and solid geometry,
Epistle in tatters . . .

————————

You doom us who see your face.
You force on us your sorrow:

So frail and vile throughout,

                    as ours is,

It assails the ear like paradise.

The moon goes up and goes down,

                                roused and quenched low.

You bend like a calling card away from the dawn.

You doom us who see your face.

                ——————

It's the mind, not the body,

That bears us up and shines a light in our eyes:

If spirit is nothingness,

                  I'd rather the light came back than the light came on.

                ——————

Noon, and you're there again on the other side of the sky.

Two kites have nested in the dry skirt

Of the palm tree

                    and scrape their voices like fingernails

Against the windowpane of the air

When they flutter down, quick fingers, to feed their chicks.

You'd like it on this side, I think.

                        Summer is everywhere, your favorite,

And dirt still crumbles and falls like small rain from the hand.

The wind blows in from the sea.

The girls are pretty and everyone is sad.

                ——————

The night is clear and incised,

The moon like a gold record

                  above the houses and avocado grove,

And you're back,

                floating behind the star's stitching,

Such fine thread to sip through.

Do you remember the pain of the way it was for you,

Teresa's song scratching the scab off your own youth

And approaching end,

The days not long enough, and the nights not long enough
For you to suffer it all?

                        You'd do the same again, I'll bet,
And live the same life,
Paper umbrella above your head
To keep the snow off,

          the color of snowfall like curtains across your eyes.

———————

Not one word has ever melted in glory not one.
We keep on sending them up, however,
As the sun rains down.

                   You did it yourself,
All those nights looking up at the sky, wanting to be there
Away from the grief of being here
In the wrong flesh.
They must look funny to you now,
Rising like smoke signals into the infinite,
The same letter over and over,

                       big o and little o.

———————

August 15th, and ten days
And 1700 miles from where we last spoke, less than a twitch
For you,

         70 years into the past for me
As the crow flies and the weather burns.
And even here, like the hand of a drowning man, your own
   hand
Points out from behind the stars

                  still without urgency
The Bear and the dark waters
Each boat of flesh sets sail on . . .
Such hurt, and I turn the page

           to this place, built in 1912
By someone who'd never heard your name

But knew your face on clear nights
over Mt. Caribou
As you wheeled west, your mouth full of stars.

_____

That's all I wanted to say.
Think of me now and then, as I think of you
When the moon's like a golden tick on the summer sky
Gorged with light:
you're part of my parts of speech.
Think of me now and then. I'll think of you.

LOOKING AT PICTURES

How many times have I come here
                        to look at these photographs
And reproductions of all I've thought most beautiful
In the natural world,
And tried to enter the tired bodies assembled in miniature?

St. Francis, for instance, who saw the fire in the pig's mouth,
And trees full of the drowned
                    who forgot to cross themselves.
Or the last half-page of the Verse of Light in Arabic
                             torn from the Koran,
Tacked like a terrible crystal this side of the reading lamp.
Beside it Adam and Eve in agony
Are ushered out through the stone gates of Paradise.

On the other side of the room
A Fra Angelico angel beats time on a tambourine:
Everything's music to his ears.
                       And Rothko has a black-on-red
Painting below it I'd sink through flat on my back
Endlessly down into nothingness . . .

But not now. Not now when the hound of the Pope's men
Is leaping, not now
                when the banner of St. George
Dragontails out of the sky. Not now
When our fathers stand in their riding boots, arms crossed,
Trying to tell us something we can't quite hear,
                      our ears jugged like Kafka's.

The devil eats us, I know, but our arms don't touch his neck.
Help me remember, Madonna of Tenderness,
                              that everything slides away
Into him stealthily.

St. Francis is feeding the birds again.
And someone with wings and brown hair
                              is telling Mary something
Again in a different dress.

St. Anne and Château Noir,
The flute player from 2200 B.C.
Out of the Cyclades—St. Ignatius Loyola
                              would find no rope in all this
To cinch around himself. It's synaptical here,
And rearranged.

We stare at the backs of our own heads continually
Walking in cadence into the past,
Great-grandfathers before their suicides,
                              Venice in sunshine, Venice in rain,
Someone standing in front of the sea
                              watching the waves come in . . .

CALIFORNIA DREAMING

We are not born yet, and everything's crystal under our feet.
We are not brethren, we are not underlings.
We are another nation,

                    living by voices that you will never hear,
Caught in the net of splendor

                         of time-to-come on the earth.
We shine in our distant chambers, we are golden.

———————

Midmorning, and Darvon dustfall off the Pacific
Stuns us to ecstasy,

                  October sun
Stuck like a tack on the eastern drift of the sky,
The idea of God on the other,

                     body by body
Rinsed in the Sunday prayer-light, draining away
Into the undercoating and slow sparks of the west,

                    which is our solitude and our joy.

———————

I've looked at this ridge of lights for six years now

                      and still don't like it,
Strung out like Good Friday along a cliff
That Easters down to the ocean,
A dark wing with ruffled feathers as far out as Catalina
Fallen from some sky,

                 ruffled and laid back by the wind,
Santa Ana that lisps its hot breath

               on the neck of everything.

———————

What if the soul indeed is outside the body,

              a little rainfall of light

Moistening our every step, prismatic, apotheosizic?
What if inside the body another shape is waiting to come out,
White as a quilt, loose as a fever,
                              and sways in the easy tides there?
What other anagoge in this life but the self?
What other ladder to Paradise
                              but the smooth handholds of the rib cage?
High in the palm tree the orioles twitter and grieve.
We twitter and grieve, the spider twirls the honey bee,
Who twitters and grieves, around in her net,
                              then draws it by one leg
Up to the fishbone fern leaves inside the pepper tree
                              swaddled in silk
And turns it again and again until it is shining.

———————

Some nights, when the rock-and-roll band next door has quit
   playing,
And the last helicopter has thwonked back to the Marine base,
And the dark lets all its weight down
                              to within a half inch of the ground,
I sit outside in the gold lamé of the moon
                              as the town sleeps and the country sleeps
Like flung confetti around me,
And wonder just what in the hell I'm doing out here
So many thousands of miles away from what I know best.
And what I know best
                              has nothing to do with Point Conception
And Avalon and the long erasure of ocean
Out there where the landscape ends.
What I know best is a little thing.
It sits on the far side of the simile,
                              the like that's like the like.

———————

Today is sweet stuff on the tongue.
The question of how we should live our lives in this world

Will find no answer from us

                     this morning,
Sunflick, the ocean humping its back
Beneath us, shivering out

                    wave after wave we fall from
And cut through in a white scar of healed waters,
Our wet suits glossed slick as seals,

                    our boards grown sharp as cries.
We rise and fall like the sun.

———————

Ghost of the Muse and her dogsbody
Suspended above the beach, November 25,
Sun like a Valium disc, smog like rust in the trees.
White-hooded and friar-backed,

               a gull choir eyeballs the wave reach.
Invisibly pistoned, the sea keeps it up,

           plunges and draws back, plunges and draws back,
Yesterday hung like a porcelain cup behind the eyes,
Sonorous valves, insistent extremities,

             the worm creeping out of the heart . . .

———————

Who are these people we pretend to be,

                untouched by the setting sun?
They stand less stiffly than we do, and handsomer,
First on the left foot, and then the right.
Just for a moment we see ourselves inside them,

                   peering out,
And then they go their own way and we go ours,
Back to the window seat above the driveway,
Christmas lights in the pepper tree,

              black Madonna
Gazing out from the alicanthus.
Chalk eyes downcast, heavy with weeping and bitterness,
Her time has come round again.

———————

Piece by small piece the world falls away from us like spores
From a milkweed pod,
                    and everything we have known,
And everyone we have known,
Is taken away by the wind to forgetfulness,
Somebody always humming,
                         California dreaming . . .

NOTES

ABOUT THE AUTHOR

CHARLES WRIGHT was born in Pickwick Dam, Tennessee, in 1935 and was educated at Davidson College and the University of Iowa. He and his family live in Charlottesville, where he teaches at the University of Virginia.

Mr. Wright received the Edgar Allan Poe Award administered by the Academy of American Poets in 1976 and an Academy-Institute Grant from the American Academy and Institute of Arts and Letters in 1977. His translation of the Italian poet Eugenio Montale's *The Storm and Other Things* won the 1978 P.E.N. Translation Prize. *Country Music: Selected Early Poems* was co-winner of the 1983 American Book Award in poetry.